PLEASE SIGN OUR GUEST BOOK

Celebrating

On This Date

GUEST

Name:

Address:

Email:

MESSAGE

GUEST

Name:

Address:

Email:

MESSAGE

GUEST

Name:

Address:

Email:

MESSAGE

GUEST

Name:

Address:

Email:

MESSAGE

GUEST

Name:

Address:

Email:

MESSAGE

GUEST

Name:

Address:

Email:

MESSAGE

GUEST

Name:

Address:

Email:

MESSAGE

GUEST

Name:

Address:

Email:

MESSAGE

GUEST

Name:

Address:

Email:

MESSAGE

GUEST

Name:

Address:

Email:

MESSAGE

GUEST

Name:

Address:

Email:

MESSAGE

GUEST

Name:

Address:

Email:

MESSAGE

GUEST

Name: __________

Address: __________

Email: __________

MESSAGE

GUEST

Name: __________

Address: __________

Email: __________

MESSAGE

GUEST

Name: __________

Address: __________

Email: __________

MESSAGE

GUEST

Name:

Address:

Email:

MESSAGE

GUEST

Name:

Address:

Email:

MESSAGE

GUEST

Name:

Address:

Email:

MESSAGE

GUEST

Name:

Address:

Email:

MESSAGE

GUEST

Name:

Address:

Email:

MESSAGE

GUEST

Name:

Address:

Email:

MESSAGE

GUEST

Name: ______________________

Address: ______________________

____

Email: ______________________

MESSAGE

____

____

____

____

GUEST

Name: ______________________

Address: ______________________

____

Email: ______________________

MESSAGE

____

____

____

____

GUEST

Name: ______________________

Address: ______________________

____

Email: ______________________

MESSAGE

____

____

____

____

GUEST

Name: ______________________

Address: ______________________

____

Email: ______________________

MESSAGE

____

____

____

____

GUEST

Name: ______________________

Address: ______________________

____

Email: ______________________

MESSAGE

____

____

____

____

GUEST

Name: ______________________

Address: ______________________

____

Email: ______________________

MESSAGE

____

____

____

____

GUEST

Name:

Address:

Email:

MESSAGE

GUEST

Name:

Address:

Email:

MESSAGE

GUEST

Name:

Address:

Email:

MESSAGE

GUEST

Name: ______

Address: ______

______

Email: ______

MESSAGE

______

______

______

______

GUEST

Name: ______

Address: ______

______

Email: ______

MESSAGE

______

______

______

______

GUEST

Name: ______

Address: ______

______

Email: ______

MESSAGE

______

______

______

______

GUEST

Name:

Address:

Email:

MESSAGE

GUEST

Name:

Address:

Email:

MESSAGE

GUEST

Name:

Address:

Email:

MESSAGE

GUEST

Name:

Address:

Email:

MESSAGE

GUEST

Name:

Address:

Email:

MESSAGE

GUEST

Name:

Address:

Email:

MESSAGE

GUEST

Name:

Address:

Email:

MESSAGE

GUEST

Name:

Address:

Email:

MESSAGE

GUEST

Name:

Address:

Email:

MESSAGE

GUEST

Name:

Address:

Email:

MESSAGE

GUEST

Name:

Address:

Email:

MESSAGE

GUEST

Name:

Address:

Email:

MESSAGE

GUEST

Name: ______

Address: ______

______

Email: ______

MESSAGE

______

______

______

______

GUEST

Name: ______

Address: ______

______

Email: ______

MESSAGE

______

______

______

______

GUEST

Name: ______

Address: ______

______

Email: ______

MESSAGE

______

______

______

______

GUEST

Name: ______

Address: ______

______

Email: ______

MESSAGE

______

______

______

______

GUEST

Name: ______

Address: ______

______

Email: ______

MESSAGE

______

______

______

______

GUEST

Name: ______

Address: ______

______

Email: ______

MESSAGE

______

______

______

______

GUEST

Name:

Address:

Email:

MESSAGE

GUEST

Name:

Address:

Email:

MESSAGE

GUEST

Name:

Address:

Email:

MESSAGE

GUEST

Name:

Address:

Email:

MESSAGE

GUEST

Name:

Address:

Email:

MESSAGE

GUEST

Name:

Address:

Email:

MESSAGE

GUEST

Name:

Address:

Email:

MESSAGE

GUEST

Name:

Address:

Email:

MESSAGE

GUEST

Name:

Address:

Email:

MESSAGE

GUEST

Name: ______________________

Address: ______________________

____

Email: ______________________

MESSAGE

____

____

____

____

GUEST

Name: ______________________

Address: ______________________

____

Email: ______________________

MESSAGE

____

____

____

____

GUEST

Name: ______________________

Address: ______________________

____

Email: ______________________

MESSAGE

____

____

____

____

GUEST

Name:

Address:

Email:

MESSAGE

GUEST

Name:

Address:

Email:

MESSAGE

GUEST

Name:

Address:

Email:

MESSAGE

GUEST

Name:

Address:

Email:

MESSAGE

GUEST

Name:

Address:

Email:

MESSAGE

GUEST

Name:

Address:

Email:

MESSAGE

GUEST

Name:

Address:

Email:

MESSAGE

GUEST

Name:

Address:

Email:

MESSAGE

GUEST

Name:

Address:

Email:

MESSAGE

GUEST

Name:

Address:

Email:

MESSAGE

GUEST

Name:

Address:

Email:

MESSAGE

GUEST

Name:

Address:

Email:

MESSAGE

GUEST

Name:

Address:

Email:

MESSAGE

GUEST

Name:

Address:

Email:

MESSAGE

GUEST

Name:

Address:

Email:

MESSAGE

GUEST

Name:

Address:

Email:

MESSAGE

GUEST

Name:

Address:

Email:

MESSAGE

GUEST

Name:

Address:

Email:

MESSAGE

GUEST

Name:

Address:

Email:

MESSAGE

GUEST

Name:

Address:

Email:

MESSAGE

GUEST

Name:

Address:

Email:

MESSAGE

GUEST

Name:

Address:

Email:

MESSAGE

GUEST

Name:

Address:

Email:

MESSAGE

GUEST

Name:

Address:

Email:

MESSAGE

GUEST

Name:

Address:

Email:

MESSAGE

GUEST

Name:

Address:

Email:

MESSAGE

GUEST

Name:

Address:

Email:

MESSAGE

GUEST

Name:

Address:

Email:

MESSAGE

GUEST

Name:

Address:

Email:

MESSAGE

GUEST

Name:

Address:

Email:

MESSAGE

GUEST

Name:

Address:

Email:

MESSAGE

GUEST

Name:

Address:

Email:

MESSAGE

GUEST

Name:

Address:

Email:

MESSAGE

GUEST

Name:

Address:

Email:

MESSAGE

GUEST

Name:

Address:

Email:

MESSAGE

GUEST

Name:

Address:

Email:

MESSAGE

GUEST

Name:

Address:

Email:

MESSAGE

GUEST

Name:

Address:

Email:

MESSAGE

GUEST

Name:

Address:

Email:

MESSAGE

GUEST

Name:

Address:

Email:

MESSAGE

GUEST

Name:

Address:

Email:

MESSAGE

GUEST

Name:

Address:

Email:

MESSAGE

GUEST

Name:

Address:

Email:

MESSAGE

GUEST

Name:

Address:

Email:

MESSAGE

GUEST

Name:

Address:

Email:

MESSAGE

GUEST

Name:

Address:

Email:

MESSAGE

GUEST

Name:

Address:

Email:

MESSAGE

GUEST

Name:

Address:

Email:

MESSAGE

GUEST

Name:

Address:

Email:

MESSAGE

GUEST

Name:

Address:

Email:

MESSAGE

GUEST

Name:

Address:

Email:

MESSAGE

GUEST

Name:

Address:

Email:

MESSAGE

GUEST

Name:

Address:

Email:

MESSAGE

GUEST

Name:

Address:

Email:

MESSAGE

GUEST

Name: __________

Address: __________

Email: __________

MESSAGE

GUEST

Name:

Address:

Email:

MESSAGE

GUEST

Name:

Address:

Email:

MESSAGE

GUEST

Name:

Address:

Email:

MESSAGE

GUEST

Name:

Address:

Email:

MESSAGE

GUEST

Name:

Address:

Email:

MESSAGE

GUEST

Name:

Address:

Email:

MESSAGE

GUEST

Name:

Address:

Email:

MESSAGE

GUEST

Name:

Address:

Email:

MESSAGE

GUEST

Name:

Address:

Email:

MESSAGE

GUEST

Name:

Address:

Email:

MESSAGE

GUEST

Name:

Address:

Email:

MESSAGE

GUEST

Name:

Address:

Email:

MESSAGE

GUEST

Name:

Address:

Email:

MESSAGE

GUEST

Name:

Address:

Email:

MESSAGE

GUEST

Name:

Address:

Email:

MESSAGE

GUEST

Name:

Address:

Email:

MESSAGE

GUEST

Name:

Address:

Email:

MESSAGE

GUEST

Name:

Address:

Email:

MESSAGE

GUEST

Name:

Address:

Email:

MESSAGE

GUEST

Name:

Address:

Email:

MESSAGE

GUEST

Name:

Address:

Email:

MESSAGE

GUEST

Name:

Address:

Email:

MESSAGE

GUEST

Name:

Address:

Email:

MESSAGE

GUEST

Name:

Address:

Email:

MESSAGE

GUEST

Name:

Address:

Email:

MESSAGE

GUEST

Name:

Address:

Email:

MESSAGE

GUEST

Name:

Address:

Email:

MESSAGE

GUEST

Name:

Address:

Email:

MESSAGE

GUEST

Name:

Address:

Email:

MESSAGE

GUEST

Name:

Address:

Email:

MESSAGE

GUEST

Name:

Address:

Email:

MESSAGE

GUEST

Name:

Address:

Email:

MESSAGE

GUEST

Name:

Address:

Email:

MESSAGE

GUEST

Name:

Address:

Email:

MESSAGE

GUEST

Name:

Address:

Email:

MESSAGE

GUEST

Name: ______________________

Address: ______________________

____

Email: ______________________

MESSAGE

____

____

____

____

GUEST

Name: ______________________

Address: ______________________

____

Email: ______________________

MESSAGE

____

____

____

____

GUEST

Name: ______________________

Address: ______________________

____

Email: ______________________

MESSAGE

____

____

____

____

GUEST

Name:

Address:

Email:

MESSAGE

GUEST

Name:

Address:

Email:

MESSAGE

GUEST

Name:

Address:

Email:

MESSAGE

GUEST

Name:

Address:

Email:

MESSAGE

GUEST

Name:

Address:

Email:

MESSAGE

GUEST

Name:

Address:

Email:

MESSAGE

GUEST

Name:

Address:

Email:

MESSAGE

GUEST

Name:

Address:

Email:

MESSAGE

GUEST

Name:

Address:

Email:

MESSAGE

GUEST

Name: ______________________________

Address: ______________________________

____

Email: ______________________________

MESSAGE

____

____

____

____

GUEST

Name: ______________________________

Address: ______________________________

____

Email: ______________________________

MESSAGE

____

____

____

____

GUEST

Name: ______________________________

Address: ______________________________

____

Email: ______________________________

MESSAGE

____

____

____

____

GUEST

Name:

Address:

Email:

MESSAGE

GUEST

Name:

Address:

Email:

MESSAGE

GUEST

Name:

Address:

Email:

MESSAGE

GUEST

Name:

Address:

Email:

MESSAGE

GUEST

Name:

Address:

Email:

MESSAGE

GUEST

Name:

Address:

Email:

MESSAGE

GUEST

Name:

Address:

Email:

MESSAGE

GUEST

Name:

Address:

Email:

MESSAGE

GUEST

Name:

Address:

Email:

MESSAGE

GUEST

Name:

Address:

Email:

MESSAGE

GUEST

Name:

Address:

Email:

MESSAGE

GUEST

Name:

Address:

Email:

MESSAGE

GUEST

Name:

Address:

Email:

MESSAGE

GUEST

Name:

Address:

Email:

MESSAGE

GUEST

Name:

Address:

Email:

MESSAGE

GUEST

Name:

Address:

Email:

MESSAGE

GUEST

Name:

Address:

Email:

MESSAGE

GUEST

Name:

Address:

Email:

MESSAGE

GUEST

Name:

Address:

Email:

MESSAGE

GUEST

Name:

Address:

Email:

MESSAGE

GUEST

Name:

Address:

Email:

MESSAGE

GUEST

Name:

Address:

Email:

MESSAGE

GUEST

Name:

Address:

Email:

MESSAGE

GUEST

Name:

Address:

Email:

MESSAGE

GUEST

Name: ______________________________

Address: ______________________________

____

Email: ______________________________

MESSAGE

____

____

____

____

GUEST

Name: ______________________________

Address: ______________________________

____

Email: ______________________________

MESSAGE

____

____

____

____

GUEST

Name: ______________________________

Address: ______________________________

____

Email: ______________________________

MESSAGE

____

____

____

____

GUEST

Name:

Address:

Email:

MESSAGE

GUEST

Name:

Address:

Email:

MESSAGE

GUEST

Name:

Address:

Email:

MESSAGE

GUEST

Name:

Address:

Email:

MESSAGE

GUEST

Name:

Address:

Email:

MESSAGE

GUEST

Name:

Address:

Email:

MESSAGE

GUEST

Name:

Address:

Email:

MESSAGE

GUEST

Name:

Address:

Email:

MESSAGE

GUEST

Name:

Address:

Email:

MESSAGE

GUEST

Name:

Address:

Email:

MESSAGE

GUEST

Name:

Address:

Email:

MESSAGE

GUEST

Name:

Address:

Email:

MESSAGE

GUEST

Name:

Address:

Email:

MESSAGE

GUEST

Name:

Address:

Email:

MESSAGE

GUEST

Name:

Address:

Email:

MESSAGE

GUEST

Name: ______

Address: ______

______

Email: ______

MESSAGE

______

______

______

______

GUEST

Name: ______

Address: ______

______

Email: ______

MESSAGE

______

______

______

______

GUEST

Name: ______

Address: ______

______

Email: ______

MESSAGE

______

______

______

______

GUEST

Name:

Address:

Email:

MESSAGE

GUEST

Name:

Address:

Email:

MESSAGE

GUEST

Name:

Address:

Email:

MESSAGE

GUEST

Name:

Address:

Email:

MESSAGE

GUEST

Name:

Address:

Email:

MESSAGE

GUEST

Name:

Address:

Email:

MESSAGE

GUEST

Name:

Address:

Email:

MESSAGE

GUEST

Name:

Address:

Email:

MESSAGE

GUEST

Name:

Address:

Email:

MESSAGE

GUEST

Name:

Address:

Email:

MESSAGE

GUEST

Name:

Address:

Email:

MESSAGE

GUEST

Name:

Address:

Email:

MESSAGE

GUEST

Name:

Address:

Email:

MESSAGE

GUEST

Name:

Address:

Email:

MESSAGE

GUEST

Name:

Address:

Email:

MESSAGE

GUEST

Name:

Address:

Email:

MESSAGE

GUEST

Name:

Address:

Email:

MESSAGE

GUEST

Name:

Address:

Email:

MESSAGE

GUEST

Name:

Address:

Email:

MESSAGE

GUEST

Name:

Address:

Email:

MESSAGE

GUEST

Name:

Address:

Email:

MESSAGE

GUEST

Name: ______________________

Address: ______________________

____

Email: ______________________

MESSAGE

____

____

____

____

GUEST

Name: ______________________

Address: ______________________

____

Email: ______________________

MESSAGE

____

____

____

____

GUEST

Name: ______________________

Address: ______________________

____

Email: ______________________

MESSAGE

____

____

____

____

GUEST

Name:

Address:

Email:

MESSAGE

GUEST

Name:

Address:

Email:

MESSAGE

GUEST

Name:

Address:

Email:

MESSAGE

GUEST

Name: ____________________

Address: ____________________

____

Email: ____________________

MESSAGE

GUEST

Name: ____________________

Address: ____________________

____

Email: ____________________

MESSAGE

GUEST

Name: ____________________

Address: ____________________

____

Email: ____________________

MESSAGE

GUEST

Name:

Address:

Email:

MESSAGE

GUEST

Name:

Address:

Email:

MESSAGE

GUEST

Name:

Address:

Email:

MESSAGE

GUEST

Name:

Address:

Email:

MESSAGE

GUEST

Name:

Address:

Email:

MESSAGE

GUEST

Name:

Address:

Email:

MESSAGE

GUEST

Name:

Address:

Email:

MESSAGE

GUEST

Name:

Address:

Email:

MESSAGE

GUEST

Name:

Address:

Email:

MESSAGE

GUEST

Name:

Address:

Email:

MESSAGE

GUEST

Name:

Address:

Email:

MESSAGE

GUEST

Name:

Address:

Email:

MESSAGE

GUEST

Name:

Address:

Email:

MESSAGE

GUEST

Name:

Address:

Email:

MESSAGE

GUEST

Name:

Address:

Email:

MESSAGE

GUEST

Name:

Address:

Email:

MESSAGE

GUEST

Name:

Address:

Email:

MESSAGE

GUEST

Name:

Address:

Email:

MESSAGE

GUEST

Name:

Address:

Email:

MESSAGE

GUEST

Name:

Address:

Email:

MESSAGE

GUEST

Name:

Address:

Email:

MESSAGE

GUEST

Name:

Address:

Email:

MESSAGE

GUEST

Name:

Address:

Email:

MESSAGE

GUEST

Name:

Address:

Email:

MESSAGE

GUEST

Name: ____________________

Address: ____________________

____

Email: ____________________

MESSAGE

____

____

____

____

GUEST

Name: ____________________

Address: ____________________

____

Email: ____________________

MESSAGE

____

____

____

____

GUEST

Name: ____________________

Address: ____________________

____

Email: ____________________

MESSAGE

____

____

____

____

GUEST

Name: ______________________

Address: ______________________

____

Email: ______________________

MESSAGE

____

____

____

____

GUEST

Name: ______________________

Address: ______________________

____

Email: ______________________

MESSAGE

____

____

____

____

GUEST

Name: ______________________

Address: ______________________

____

Email: ______________________

MESSAGE

____

____

____

____

GUEST

Name: ______________________

Address: ______________________

____

Email: ______________________

MESSAGE

____

____

____

____

GUEST

Name: ______________________

Address: ______________________

____

Email: ______________________

MESSAGE

____

____

____

____

GUEST

Name: ______________________

Address: ______________________

____

Email: ______________________

MESSAGE

____

____

____

____

GUEST

Name:

Address:

Email:

MESSAGE

GUEST

Name:

Address:

Email:

MESSAGE

GUEST

Name:

Address:

Email:

MESSAGE

GUEST

Name: ______________________

Address: ______________________

____

Email: ______________________

MESSAGE

____

____

____

____

GUEST

Name: ______________________

Address: ______________________

____

Email: ______________________

MESSAGE

____

____

____

____

GUEST

Name: ______________________

Address: ______________________

____

Email: ______________________

MESSAGE

____

____

____

____

GUEST

Name:

Address:

Email:

MESSAGE

GUEST

Name:

Address:

Email:

MESSAGE

GUEST

Name:

Address:

Email:

MESSAGE

GUEST

Name: ______

Address: ______

______

Email: ______

MESSAGE

______

______

______

______

GUEST

Name: ______

Address: ______

______

Email: ______

MESSAGE

______

______

______

______

GUEST

Name: ______

Address: ______

______

Email: ______

MESSAGE

______

______

______

______

GUEST

Name:

Address:

Email:

MESSAGE

GUEST

Name:

Address:

Email:

MESSAGE

GUEST

Name:

Address:

Email:

MESSAGE

GUEST

Name:

Address:

Email:

MESSAGE

GUEST

Name:

Address:

Email:

MESSAGE

GUEST

Name:

Address:

Email:

MESSAGE

GUEST

Name:

Address:

Email:

MESSAGE

GUEST

Name:

Address:

Email:

MESSAGE

GUEST

Name:

Address:

Email:

MESSAGE

GUEST

Name:

Address:

Email:

MESSAGE

GUEST

Name:

Address:

Email:

MESSAGE

GUEST

Name:

Address:

Email:

MESSAGE

PHOTOS & MEMENTOS

PHOTOS & MEMENTOS

PHOTOS & MEMENTOS

PHOTOS & MEMENTOS

PHOTOS & MEMENTOS

PHOTOS & MEMENTOS

PHOTOS & MEMENTOS

PHOTOS & MEMENTOS

PHOTOS & MEMENTOS

PHOTOS & MEMENTOS

PHOTOS & MEMENTOS

PHOTOS & MEMENTOS

PHOTOS & MEMENTOS

PHOTOS & MEMENTOS

PHOTOS & MEMENTOS

PHOTOS & MEMENTOS

PHOTOS & MEMENTOS

PHOTOS & MEMENTOS

PHOTOS & MEMENTOS

PHOTOS & MEMENTOS

PHOTOS & MEMENTOS

PHOTOS & MEMENTOS

PHOTOS & MEMENTOS

PHOTOS & MEMENTOS

PHOTOS & MEMENTOS

PHOTOS & MEMENTOS

PHOTOS & MEMENTOS

PHOTOS & MEMENTOS

PHOTOS & MEMENTOS

PHOTOS & MEMENTOS

PHOTOS & MEMENTOS

PHOTOS & MEMENTOS

PHOTOS & MEMENTOS

PHOTOS & MEMENTOS

PHOTOS & MEMENTOS

PHOTOS & MEMENTOS

PHOTOS & MEMENTOS

PHOTOS & MEMENTOS

PHOTOS & MEMENTOS

PHOTOS & MEMENTOS

PHOTOS & MEMENTOS

PHOTOS & MEMENTOS

PHOTOS & MEMENTOS

"I have spent many happy evenings without understanding a word."

THE DOWAGER COUNTESS

DOWNTON ABBEY

INSIGHTS
www.insighteditions.com

MANUFACTURED IN CHINA
10 9 8 7 6 5 4 3 2 1